ONCE UPON A PUMPKIN

50 CREATIVE PUMPKIN SEASONED, FLAVORED, SHAPED & SPICED RECIPES

MAGGIE MICHALCZYK, RD

ISBN: 0-692-18406-6
ISBN-13: 978-0-692-18406-6

Sponsors of this book include Simple Mills, Libby's, Quaker, siggi's dairy, and Gilbert's Craft Sausages. I'm proud to partner with these amazing brands to bring you recipes highlighting their delicious pumpkin products and products that pair well with pumpkin. I hope that you'll find them as delicious and nutritious as I do!

Follow Maggie on Instagram at @onceuponpumpkin

DEDICATION

To my sisters, Lucy and Dorothy, my parents, Barbara and Stanley, and to Rob.

You've made my wildest pumpkin dreams possible. You've shared in my joy of finding pumpkin things, ate every pumpkin food I asked you to, and scoured every pumpkin patch with me until we found the perfect pumpkin. To some this love affair with fall would have seemed crazy but I swear it was your unconditional support that always assured me I could achieve anything I set my mind to. You've each inspired me in so many different ways and made me the person that I am today. Each one of these recipes reminds me that it's the people you share them with that matters the most and there's no one I would rather celebrate this gorgeous season of life than with each one of you.

Love,

TABLE OF CONTENTS

BREAD & MUFFINS

BARS & CAKES

COOKIES

SOUPS

MAIN DISHES

PIES

SIDES

PUMPKIN SEEDS 5 WAYS

DRINKS

DOG TREATS

DIETARY RESTRICTIONS? NO PROBLEM!

Throughout the book, you'll see small colored pumpkins next to the recipes. These pumpkins will help you easily find recipes that will fit common dietary restrictions.

 GLUTEN-FREE

 DAIRY-FREE

 PALEO FRIENDLY

 VEGAN

30 WAYS TO USE A CAN OF PUMPKIN

QUESADILLAS Mix 1/2 cup pumpkin and 1 tablespoon adobo sauce (from a can of chipotle chiles). Spread on tortillas and top with shredded cheddar cheddar cheese, chicken, sautéed spinach & mushrooms. Top with second tortilla and sauté on a pan until crispy and golden brown.

MASHED SWEET POTATOES Cook 2 lbs. potatoes and mash with 1 cup pumpkin, 1 sprig of sage, and ¼ teaspoon nutmeg.

DEVILED EGGS Halve 12 hard-boiled eggs. Mash yolks with ½ cup pumpkin and 0% plain Greek yogurt, 1 tsp. Dijon mustard, ½ tsp. salt and ground coriander. Spoon into egg whites.

MUSTARD Mix 2 tbsp. each pumpkin, grainy mustard, and honey.

VINAIGRETTE Whisk 2 tbsp. each apple cider vinegar and pumpkin and 1 tsp. Dijon mustard; whisk in 1/4 cup extra-virgin olive oil. Add a pinch of salt, pepper and red pepper flakes for a kick.

APPLESAUCE Simmer 4 chopped peeled apples, 1 cup water, 1/2 cup pumpkin, and 1/2 cup sugar or coconut sugar, the juice of one lemon and a cinnamon stick. Stir occasionally, mashing with a fork for 12 minutes.

HOT COCOA Stir together 1 cup hot water with 2 tbsp. cocoa powder. Add 2 tbsp. pumpkin and a dash of pumpkin pie spice.

PASTA SAUCE Stir 1 cup pumpkin into 2 cups of your favorite pasta sauce.

YOGURT Stir together ¼ cup pumpkin with 0% plain Greek yogurt and 1 tsp. pumpkin pie spice.

SMOOTHIE Add ¼ cup pumpkin to your favorite smoothie combination to thicken the texture and add more nutrition!

OATMEAL Simmer 1½ cup unsweetened almond milk with 1 cup old fashioned oats, ½ cup pumpkin, 2 tsp. pumpkin pie spice and a splash of vanilla extract until creamy. Top with sliced almonds, pecans, banana slices, berries or a heaping tablespoon of nut butter.

CHIA PUDDING Mix together ¼ cup chia seeds, 1¼ cup unsweetened almond milk, ¾ cup pumpkin, 1 tsp. vanilla, and 1 tbsp. maple syrup and pumpkin pie spice. Refrigerate for at least 2 hours or overnight. Top with chopped pecans, banana slices, or berries.

PUDDING In a small bowl, combine ¾ cup sugar, ½ tsp. salt, and 1 tsp. pumpkin pie spice. Beat 2 eggs in a larger bowl and add 1 1/2 cup pumpkin puree. Slowly add the sugar-spice mixture and 1¼ cup of evaporated milk. Pour mixture into a glass baking dish at 350°F. Baking times will vary depending on the size of the dish. Bake until a toothpick inserted into the center comes out clean.

TAPENADE In a food processor, combine 1 cup pumpkin with ½ cup kalamata olives, ⅓ cup sundried tomatoes (not packed in oil), 2 cloves of finely chopped garlic, 1 tbsp. of basil, and ¼ cup extra-virgin olive oil. Pulse, and add salt and pepper to taste. Serve on top of crusty Italian bread or grilled chicken.

ICE CUBES Store left over canned pumpkin in an ice cube tray and freeze. Pop cubes into future soups and smoothies!

CREAM CHEESE Mix ½ cup pumpkin with 1 package ⅓ less fat cream cheese or dairy-free cream cheese. Add 2 tbsp. honey and 1 tbsp. pumpkin pie spice.

MILKSHAKE Blend ½ cup pumpkin puree with ¼ cup milk of choice, ½ banana, and ¾ cup your favorite vanilla ice cream until smooth. Pour into a glass and top with whipped cream and graham cracker crumbles.

FOR A DOG'S UPSET STOMACH Soothe your pup's tummy troubles with the power of pumpkin! Give smaller dogs ½ teaspoon of canned pumpkin, and larger dogs approximately 1 tablespoon.

CHILI Add 1 can of pumpkin puree into your classic chili recipe and continue simmering until incorporated.

FACE MASK Whisk together ¼ cup pumpkin puree, ¼ cup Greek yogurt, 2 tbsp. raw honey, and1 tsp. cinnamon. Smooth a generous amount over your face and leave on for 15-20 minutes until almost dried. Store in an airtight container in the fridge.

SUGAR SCRUB Combine ½ cup brown sugar, 2 tbsp. pumpkin puree, 2 tbsp. coconut oil, 2 tsp. pumpkin pie spice, 1 tsp. vanilla extract. Rub into hands and feet and rinse to reveal smooth skin!

PUMPKIN CAULIFLOWER AND GARLIC MASH

INGREDIENTS

1 medium head cauliflower, broken into florets (about 6 cups)
3 garlic cloves
⅓ cup spreadable cream cheese
1 can (15 ounces) solid-pack pumpkin
1 tablespoon minced fresh thyme
1 teaspoon salt
¼ teaspoon cayenne pepper
¼ teaspoon pepper

DIRECTIONS

1) Place 1 in. of water in a large saucepan; bring to a boil. Add cauliflower and garlic cloves; cook, covered, 8-10 minutes or until tender. Drain; transfer to a food processor.

2) Add remaining ingredients; process until smooth. Return to pan; heat through, stirring occasionally.

PUMPKIN PIE SHOTS Combine 2 oz. rum or vodka (pumpkin spice flavored if you can find it!) with Rumchata and rim the glass with cinnamon sugar.

SLOPPY JOES Stir 1 cup of pumpkin puree into beef sloppy joe mixture until incorporated. Serve on top of sweet potatoes for an extra seasonal twist.

ALFREDO SAUCE Heat 2 tbsp. of butter over medium heat, add 3 cloves of minced garlic, 2 cups heavy whipping cream, and 1 cup pumpkin puree. Simmer to thicken then add ½ cup parmesan cheese and mix until well combined.

TWICE BAKED POTATO While potatoes are still warm, cut in half and scoop out the insides and place into a bowl. Save the potato skins. Over medium heat, sauté 2 tbsp. butter, ½ shallot (minced), ¼ cup scallions (chopped). Add 1 cup pumpkin, ⅔ cup parmesan cheese, and ½ cup milk and. Stir together, then reduce heat and add salt and pepper to taste and a pinch of nutmeg. Fold the mixture into the potatoes and spoon back into potato shells. Serve with extra parmesan cheese and scallions on top.

PALEO PUMPKIN MUG CAKE Combine 2 tbsp. pumpkin puree, 2 tbsp. coconut flour or almond flour, 1 egg beaten, ¼ tsp. baking soda, 1 tsp. pumpkin pie spice, ½ tsp. vanilla and a splash of maple syrup in a mug or small ramekin. Microwave for about a minute and a half. Enjoy with fruit on top!

POPSICLES In a small bowl combine 1 cup pumpkin puree, 1 tbsp. maple syrup or honey, and 1 tsp. pumpkin pie spice. In another small bowl, combine 1½ cup Greek yogurt, and ½ cup milk of choice. Layer the yogurt and pumpkin mixture in popsicle molds until they are full. Freeze for at least 6 hours.

WAFFLES Add ½ cup pumpkin puree to your favorite waffle mix for an extra moist texture and light orange color.

SPICE

THE BASICS

DIY PUMPKIN SPICE

Skip the storebought and bottle your own magic by making pumpkin pie spice at home. It's so easy to make and you'll love sprinkling it on everything this fall.

INGREDIENTS

3 tbsp. ground cinnamon
2 tsp. ground ginger
1 tsp. ground allspice
1½ tsp. ground nutmeg
½ tsp. ground cloves

DIRECTIONS

1) Mix spice together and store in an airtight container.

2) Sprinkle generously on everything all fall long!

Makes about ¼ cup

The spices that come together to make true pumpkin pie spice in fact boast many unique nutritional properties. Cinnamon is rich in antioxidants, nutmeg contains fiber and B vitamins and ginger aids in digestion just to name a few!

PUMPKIN SPICE ALMOND BUTTER

Slather this pumpkin spice latte butter on everything from pumpkin bread to pancakes this fall. It has hints of silky pumpkin spice and refreshing espresso and will remind you of the taste of a pumpkin spice latte no matter what you put it on!

INGREDIENTS

2½ c. almonds
2 tbsp. coconut oil
1 tsp. vanilla extract
1½ tsp. pumpkin pie spice
1½ tsp. espresso powder
pinch of nutmeg

DIRECTIONS

1) In a food processor combine almonds and coconut oil. Pulse until you can see almond butter starting to form at the bottom.

2) Add in vanilla extract and pumpkin pie spice. Continue pulsing.

3) Once the almond butter is starting to look silky and smooth add in the espresso powder 1 tsp. at a time. Finish with the pinch of nutmeg.

4) Store in a glass jar in the fridge for up to one week. (Trust me when I say it will go faster than that!)

Yields 1 cup almond butter.

Pumpkin Fact:

IT TAKES 4 MONTHS TO GROW A PUMPKIN.

CASHEW PUMPKIN SEED ALMOND BUTTER

Enjoy this creamy cashew pumpkin seed almond butter as the perfect topping on all of your favorite fall treats or simply on toast with banana slices on top for a delicious breakfast!

INGREDIENTS

1 cup almonds
1 cup pumpkin seeds
¾ cup cashews
1 tsp. coconut oil
2 tsp. pumpkin pie spice

DIRECTIONS

1) Preheat oven to 325°F.

2) Spread cashews and almonds evenly on a baking sheet.

3) Roast for 10 minutes and add the pumpkin seeds to the baking sheet with the other nuts for 5 more minutes.

4) Let the nuts cool for about 10 minutes and then add to a food processor along with the pumpkin pie spice.

5) Pulse until you see a creamy consistency start to form at the bottom of the bowl,(at least 5 minutes) then add the coconut oil.

6) Continue pulsing until you get your desired consistency, about 5 more minutes.

Makes 1½ cups nut butter

PUMPKIN BREAKFAST

Pumpkin puree out of the can will last for 1 week in the fridge and up to 3 months in the freezer.

HEALTHY PSL

Coffee house versions may look appealing but they often contain enough calories to be a meal and an absurd amount of sugar. Make your own at home in just a few easy steps and enjoy the delightful taste pumpkin spice in a healthier way!

INGREDIENTS

8 oz. brewed coffee
1 tbsp. LIBBY'S® 100% Pure Pumpkin
2 tbsp. CARNATION® Almond Cooking Milk
½ tsp. vanilla
½ tsp. pumpkin pie spice
Sprinkle of nutmeg
Whipped cream or whipped coconut cream to use as topping (optional)

DIRECTIONS

1) Combine all ingredients in a blender and blend until smooth.

2) Transfer to a small saucepan and heat on medium to low for about 5 minutes.

3) Pour into coffee mug and top with whipped cream if you choose and sprinkles of nutmeg.

4) Sip slowly and savor the flavors of fall!

Makes 1 cup

PUMPKIN TOAST

No matter how you slice it, pumpkin toast is a good idea! Whether savory or sweet, spreading pumpkin puree on toast will give it extra fiber and a hearty fall flavor.

INGREDIENTS

2 slices of your favorite toast
4 tbsp. LIBBY'S® 100% Pure Pumpkin

Toppings:
eggs
blueberries
pepitas
pine nuts
Parmesan cheese

DIRECTIONS

1) Toast bread and spread 2 tbsp. pumpkin puree on top of each slice.

2) Top with the different toppings for one savory slice and one sweet!

Makes 2 slices.

Pumpkin Fact:

PUMPKINS ARE TECHNICALLY A FRUIT.

PUMPKIN SPICE OVERNIGHT (COLD CREAMY) OATS

Wake up on a cool fall morning to the taste of thick and creamy, cold oats with all the fixings. Pumpkin puree adds texture and thickness to this oatmeal that practically makes itself in your fridge while you're sleeping!

INGREDIENTS

⅓ cup old-fashioned rolled oats
⅓ cup unsweetened almond milk
¼ cup pumpkin puree
2 tsp. pumpkin pie spice
1 tsp. freshly ground ginger
2 tbsp. hemp seeds
apple slices, banana, walnuts, & pumpkin seeds for topping

DIRECTIONS

1) Place the oats, almond milk, pumpkin puree, pumpkin pie spice, and fresh ginger in a bowl or a jar. Mix thoroughly to combine.

2) Cover and refrigerate overnight or for at least 5 hours.

3) In the morning, top with apple and banana slices, hemp seeds, walnuts or your favorite nut and a drizzle of peanut butter.

Makes 1 serving

Fresh ginger enhances the aroma of these pumpkin oats and helps to soothe the stomach.

Oats are a good source of fiber and can help support a healthy digestive system.

SAVORY PUMPKIN & GINGER OAT BOWL

Explore the savory side of oatmeal with this tangy, pumpkin ginger oat bowl made with Quaker oats! The bowl of oats topped with an egg is a fun and delicious way to incorporate vegetables into your morning, not to mention giving you the protein and fiber to help fuel your morning.

INGREDIENTS

½ cup Quaker Old Fashioned Oats
¾ cup unsweetened almond milk
½ cup pumpkin puree
1 cup spinach
2 tsp. freshly grated ginger
1½ tsp. pumpkin pie spice
pinch of nutmeg
1 egg

DIRECTIONS

1) In a small saucepan, heat oats with almond milk and pumpkin puree, stirring together until incorporated and oats begin to absorb the liquid.

2) Stir in ginger, nutmeg, and pumpkin pie spice, along with spinach until spinach is slightly wilted.

3) Remove from heat and transfer oats to bowl.

4) Cook egg sunny side up, until whites are set.

5) Top oat bowl with egg and enjoy!

Makes 1 bowl

PUMPKIN PANCAKES

Make any fall weekend feel extra special with a stack of these fluffy pumpkin pancakes. They are fluffy and spiced to perfection with hints of nutmeg, ginger and pumpkin pie spice. No matter how you flip them, they're what's for breakfast!

INGREDIENTS

1 cup almond flour
½ cup pumpkin puree
4 tbsp. almond butter
3 eggs
1 ripe banana, mashed
2 tbsp. coconut oil + more for the pan
1 tbsp. maple syrup
2 tsp. baking powder
1 tsp. vanilla
1½ tsp. pumpkin pie spice
¼ tsp. salt

DIRECTIONS

1) In a medium bowl whisk almond flour, baking powder, pumpkin pie spice and salt.

2) In another bowl, combine pumpkin, almond butter, eggs, mashed banana, coconut oil, maple syrup and vanilla.

3) Add the wet ingredients to the dry and mix together.

4) Heat a skillet or griddle to medium-low. Add about a teaspoon of coconut oil and using a ¼ cup, measure out the skillet. (Since batter is thick you may have to spread it out to make a round pancake shape.)

5) Flip once the edges start to look golden brown and they begin to slightly bubble.

6) Cook for another 2 minutes, but don't flatten with the spatula!

7) Top with fresh berries, nut butter, or a little drizzle of maple syrup.

Makes 8 small pancakes

PUMPKIN CREPES

Take a trip to Paris from your own kitchen when you make this pumpkin crepe recipe! Perfect for breakfast or dessert--no matter how you flip them!

INGREDIENTS

For the crepes:

2 large eggs
1/4 cup butter, melted
1/4 cup pumpkin purée
2 tbsp sugar
1/2 cup + 2 tbps. almond milk
1 tbps. water
1/2 tsp vanilla
1 tsp pumpkin pie spice
sprinkle of nutmeg
tiny dash of salt
8 tbsp all-purpose flour
1 tbsp. coconut for greasing the pan

For the filling:

1/2 tsp. pumpkin pie spice
2/3 cup pumpkin puree
1 cup greek yogurt
2 oz. dark chocolate melted for the drizzle on top

DIRECTIONS

1. Combine all of the crepe ingredients in a blender, except the flour, together. Mix and add in the flour, 1 tablespoon at a time, blending just until the flour has been mixed in. Chill the crepe batter for 30 minutes in the fridge.

2. Grease a crepe pan or non-stick pan with coconut oil and heat over medium heat. Pour about 1/4 c of batter into the pan and tip and tilt pan so that the batter spreads out really thin.

3. Cook each side of the crepe for 30 seconds before loosening up the edges with a spatula, and then flipping gently with help from the spatula. Repeat with remaining crepe batter.

4. In a medium-sized bowl combine the Greek yogurt, pumpkin puree, and pumpkin pie spice.

5. Spread thin along inside of crepe. Fold in half and fold one half over to make triangles.

6. Top with sliced bananas, hemp seeds and a drizzle of dark chocolate if desired!

Makes 10 crepes

MINI PUMPKIN PASTRY TARTS

These perfectly pumpkin pastries are extra cute because they're mini! They're light and flakey with just the perfect amount of pumpkin.

INGREDIENTS

For the crust:
2 cups all-purpose flour
1 cup (2 sticks) unsalted butter, cold, cut into cubes
2 tbsp. almond milk
1 tbsp. sugar
1 tsp. salt
1 egg, whisked for brushing the dough
¼ cup pumpkin butter (I like Trader Joe's!)

For the maple glaze (optional):
1 cup powdered sugar
1 tbsp. maple syrup
1 tbsp. almond or regular milk

Makes 9 mini pastry tarts

A little filling might pop out when you make them-- it adds character!

DIRECTIONS

1) In a medium bowl, whisk together flour, sugar and salt.
2) Place the flour mixture into a food processor, add the cold butter and pulse until dough forms.
3) Roll the dough into a ball and refrigerate for 30 minutes.
4) Pre-heat the oven to 350 F. Lightly dust a clean area of your counter with flour, and roll out the dough using a rolling pin until its about 1/8 of an inch thick.
5) Using a small pumpkin cookie cutter or a rectangular cookie cutter, cut out pieces of dough and put them on a lightly greased baking sheet.
6) Use your finger to make a small thumb print on half of the mini dough cut outs and add 2 tbsp. of pumpkin butter.
7) Place another cut out directly on top of the one with the filling. To close, use a fork to make small indentations around the edges of the mini pumpkin.
8) In a small bowl, whisk the egg and add the milk. Brush this mixture on top of the pastry tarts.
9) Bake for about 20 minutes until the edges turn golden brown.
10) Combine all ingredients for glaze and drizzle over pastry tarts while they are still warm

I like eating and cooking with siggi's yogurt as
it's higher in protein and lower in sugar, with
simple ingredients like real pumpkin.

PUMPKIN & SPICE YOGURT BOWL

Creamy, thick and spiced siggi's yogurt paired with crunchy, in-season toppings make this bowl full of fall flavor. Made with simple ingredients, and not a lot of sugar, you're sure to fall in love with siggi's and this yogurt bowl all fall long.

INGREDIENTS

1 cup siggi's touch of honey whole-milk yogurt
½ cup pumpkin puree
1 tsp. pumpkin pie spice
½ of a banana, sliced
¼ cup of your favorite type of apple, diced
1-2 tbsp. almonds, roughly chopped
1 tbsp. hemp seeds
Handful of pumpkin seeds
Drizzle of peanut or almond butter

DIRECTIONS

1) Mix siggi's yogurt and pumpkin puree together in a small bowl.

2) Top with banana and apple slices, and sprinkle almonds, pumpkin and hemp seeds on top.

3) Drizzle peanut or almond butter on top and enjoy!

siggi's pumpkin & spice is available as a seasonal flavor, often in the fall. You can enjoy this yogurt bowl anytime of year by substituting it for the touch of honey whole-milk flavor

COCONUT PUMPKIN LATTE BITES

Pumpkin and coconut go together almost as much as pumpkin and spice do!

INGREDIENTS

⅓ cup whole-milk plain or vanilla siggi's yogurt
½ cup pumpkin puree
¼ cup shredded coconut + more for coating on top
10 pitted dates
2 tsp. pumpkin pie spice
2 tsp. espresso powder + more for coating on top
splash of vanilla
pinch of nutmeg

DIRECTIONS

1) Combine yogurt, pumpkin puree, dates, and coconut into food processor. Pulse for 1 minute.

2) Add vanilla, pumpkin pie spice, espresso powder and pinch of nutmeg. Pulse for a couple more minutes until all combined.

3) Roll into balls, and place extra coconut flakes and espresso in a small bowl.

4) Roll balls a second time through the coconut and espresso mixture until they have a light dusting on all sides.

5) Enjoy for a week when kept in the fridge or freeze for longer!

Makes 12 balls

Pumpkin Fact

THERE ARE OVER 45 VARIETIES OF PUMPKIN

1 Tsp 5ml

FALL IN A BALL

If you could bottle the taste of the leaves changing and the sunshine of a fall day, these balls would be it.

INGREDIENTS

½ cup almond flour
½ cup pumpkin puree
2 pitted medjool dates
¼ cup unsweetened coconut flakes
¼ cup raw cashews
¼ cup almonds
¼ cup raw pumpkin seeds
1 tbsp. ground flax seed
2 tbsp. hemp seeds
1" fresh organic ginger, peeled and grated
1½ tsp pumpkin pie spice
¼ tsp sea salt
pinch of nutmeg
2 tbsp. almond milk

DIRECTIONS

1) In a food processor, combine all ingredients except for almond milk. Pulse for about a minute.

2) Add almond milk, and continue pulsing until it looks like chunky dough has formed.

3) Roll into balls with your hands. If the dough is very sticky and hard to roll, add more almond flour (about 1 tbsp, at a time).

4) Store in an airtight container in the fridge, or freeze to enjoy all fall long!

Makes roughly 14 balls

PUMPKIN BREADS & MUFFINS

ONCE UPON A PUMPKIN BREAD

The fall season would not be complete without pumpkin bread! This paleo pumpkin bread recipe is only lightly sweetened and great for topping with fresh berries, and nut butter.

INGREDIENTS

2 cups almond flour
¼ cup coconut oil, melted
¼ cup pure maple syrup
3/4 cup canned pumpkin puree
1/4 cup almond butter
3 eggs, lightly whisked
2 tsp. baking powder
1 tsp. baking soda
2 tsp. pumpkin pie spice
½ tsp. cinnamon
¼ tsp. nutmeg
¼ tsp. sea salt

DIRECTIONS

1. Preheat oven to 350°F.

2. In a large bowl, whisk together flour, baking powder, baking soda, pumpkin pie spice, cinnamon, nutmeg and salt. Set aside.

3. In a separate bowl, whisk together eggs, coconut oil, maple syrup, pumpkin puree and almond butter.

4. Pour the wet ingredients in with the dry ingredients, mixing until there are no clumps.

5. Pour pumpkin mixture into a prepared 9x5-inch loaf pan and bake for 45 to 50 minutes, or until a toothpick inserted in the center comes out clean.

Makes 1 loaf

Pumpkin Fact:

PUMPKIN IS LOADED WITH BLOOD PRESSURE REGULATING MINERALS LIKE POTASSIUM, MAGNESIUM & IRON.

PUMPKIN BLUEBERRY MUFFINS

Blueberry and pumpkin come together to share a bond that crosses the divide between summer and fall. Juicy blueberries bursting with flavor in moist and crumbly gluten-free pumpkin muffins are what you'll what with your coffee on chilly fall mornings!

INGREDIENTS

Muffins:
½ cup almond flour
½ cup coconut flour
⅔ cup brown sugar
3 eggs
1 tbsp. baking powder
1 tbsp. pumpkin pie spice
½ cup pumpkin puree
½ cup coconut oil
1 tsp. vanilla extract
¼ tsp. salt
1 cup blueberries

Streusel topping:
2 tbsp. almond flour
1 tsp. pumpkin pie spice
4 tbsp brown sugar
2 tbsp. butter

DIRECTIONS

1) Preheat the oven to 350°F.

2) In a large bowl, stir together the almond flour, coconut flour, brown sugar, baking powder, pumpkin pie spice, and salt.

3) Stir in the eggs, pumpkin puree, coconut oil, and vanilla, until completely incorporated.

4) Fold in blueberries until just evenly incorporated.

5) Spoon the batter evenly into lined muffin cups until each one is nearly full.

6) For the streusel topping combine the flour, sugar, and pumpkin pie spice in a small bowl. Cut in butter with fork until mixture resembles coarse crumbs. Sprinkle crumbles over batter in muffin cups.

7) Bake for about 25 minutes, until an inserted toothpick comes out clean.

Yields 12 muffins.

PUMPKIN CHOCOLATE CHIP BANANA BREAD

Pumpkin and banana were meant to be together in this bread perfect for the fall! Just try resisting a warm slice right out of the oven!

INGREDIENTS

2 cups whole-wheat flour
½ cup pumpkin puree
1 cup overripe banana, mashed
1½ tsp. pumpkin pie spice
¼ cup maple syrup or honey
⅓ cup unsweetened almond milk
2 tbsp. nut butter
2 tsp vanilla extract
¾ tsp baking powder
1 tsp baking soda
1 cup chocolate chips, optional

DIRECTIONS

1) Preheat oven to 350°F and lightly grease a loaf pan with coconut oil.

2) In a large bowl, whisk together flour, baking soda and powder, pumpkin pie spice, and salt.

3) In a smaller bowl mix together all of the wet ingredients.

4) Pour the wet ingredients into the dry ingredients and mix together until dough forms.

5) Fold in chocolate chips and pour batter into loaf pan.

6) Bake for approximately 30 minutes or until toothpick inserted into the center comes out clean.

Makes 1 loaf

Pumpkin Fact:

PUMPKINS ARE GROWN ON EVERY CONTINENT EXCEPT ANTARCTICA.

GOOD
morning
PUMPKIN

PUMPKIN BARS & CAKES

Cocoa nibs are like nature's chocolate chip—they're a good source of fiber, magnesium and iron.

PUMPKIN COOKIE DOUGH BARS

I don't know about you, but I'm a cookie dough anything kind of girl all the way! Infused with pumpkin and pumpkin spice, you'll feel like your eating an indulgent treat but can rest assured knowing these cookie dough bars are gluten free and lightly sweetened!

INGREDIENTS

1½ cups cashew butter
½ cup pumpkin puree
2¼ cups almond flour
3 tbsp. almond milk
⅓ cup cacao nibs or chocolate chips
3 tbsp. maple syrup
2 tbsp. cacao powder
2 tbsp. almond or peanut butter

DIRECTIONS

1) Add cashew butter, almond flour, pumpkin puree, almond milk, maple syrup and cacao nibs to food processor and blend until creamy.

2) Line a bread pan with parchment paper and scoop about 3/4 of the dough into the pan for the bottom layer of the pumpkin cookie dough bars.

3) Add the cacao powder and almond or peanut butter to food processor with remaining dough and blend again until all combined.

4) Press chocolate layer on top of the bottom layer and add to freezer to set for about an hour.

5) Slice into bars and enjoy! Keep leftovers in fridge or in the freezer for longer.

Makes about 12 bars.

PSL-MISU

The flavors of pumpkin and espresso come together for this dessert that's a combination of tirimisu and bread pudding with all of the pumpkin flavor! Pumpkin bread soaked in coffee and rum give this treat a little extra fall attitude.

INGREDIENTS

½ loaf of your favorite pumpkin bread baked and cooled
8 oz. mascarpone cheese
1/2 cup pumpkin puree
1/2 cup + 2 tbsp. powdered sugar
2 tsp. pumpkin pie spice
1 tsp. vanilla extract
1 cup brewed coffee
2 oz. dark rum

DIRECTIONS

1) In shallow bowl, crumble pumpkin bread into small pieces. Pour coffee and rum over bread and let soak for 5-10 minutes.

2) Meanwhile, in a small bowl mix together softened mascarpone, pumpkin puree, 1/2 cup powdered sugar, pumpkin pie spice and vanilla.

3) Fill bottom of a small parfait glass with 2-3 small pieces of pumpkin bread and layer the pumpkin mixture on top. Repeat until your last layer is the pumpkin mixture.

4) Top with whipped cream, cookies crumbles or a sprinkle of cinnamon. Be sure to refrigerate if not eating right away.

Makes 5 individual parfaits

Have fun topping these parfaits with whipped cream, cookie crumbles or a sprinkle of cinnamon!

Simple Mills baking mixes are made with nutrient-dense, whole food ingredients like almonds and coconut flour.

NAKED PUMPKIN BANANA CAKE

Celebrate the season with this beautiful and delicious naked pumpkin banana cake made with *Simple Mills*! Get lost in its layers of gluten-free goodness garnished with autumn foilage--it's almost too pretty to eat!

INGREDIENTS

1 package *Simple Mills* Pumpkin Bread Mix
1 package *Simple Mills* Banana Bread Mix
2 containers *Simple Mills* Vanilla Frosting

Optional Tools:
1-2 6 x 2" round cake pans
Cake leveler
Angled icing spatula

DIRECTIONS

1) Prepare pumpkin muffin and bread mix according to instructions for bread. Pour batter into a greased 6 x 2" round cake pan and bake.

2) Remove from oven and let cool on a baking rack. Repeat steps for banana bread mix and bake while pumpkin cake is cooling.

3) Once both cakes have cooled, cut them in half horizontally so you have two equal cake halves.

4) Place one layer of the pumpkin cake onto a plate or cake stand. Use an angled icing spatula to scoop out about ¼ cup of vanilla frosting on top of cake.

5) Use the spatula to spread the icing around the top of the cake and lightly spread it on the sides so that you can still see the cake through the thin layer of frosting.

6) Place one banana layer on top and begin icing the same way. Repeat with remaining layers of pumpkin and banana.

7) Decorate the cake with garnishes like leaves or use a small pumpkin as a topper.

It takes 4 months to grow a pumpkin.

PUMPKIN CHEESECAKE

I make this pumpkin cheesecake every year for my family as our Thanksgiving dessert, and I hope you enjoy it just as much as we do! To me it symbolizes thankfulness and gratitude for the love, laughter, exciting experiences, tough times and beautiful moments brought about in the past year. Enjoying it with the people sitting around you is truly the biggest blessing of all!

INGREDIENTS

1 cup graham cracker crumbs
2 tbsp. butter, melted
3 packages cream cheese, softened
¾ cup sugar
¼ cup dark rum
2 tsp. vanilla extract
4 eggs
1 can LIBBY'S® 100% Pure Pumpkin
2 tbsp. cornstarch
1½ tsp. pumpkin pie spice
½ tsp. salt
⅔ cup CARNATION® Evaporated Milk

DIRECTIONS

1) Pre heat oven to 325°F.
2) Combine graham cracker crumbs with butter. Mix until combined.
3) Press onto bottom and 1 inch up side of 9-inch springform pan.
4) Bake for 10 minutes and let cool completely.
5) Meanwhile, in a medium bowl, beat the softened cream cheese until smooth (1 minute). Add the sugar and beat until combined.
6) Add the vanilla and the rum. Lastly, add eggs one at a time until just combined. Don't over beat!
7) In a separate bowl, combine pumpkin, cornstarch, pumpkin pie spice and salt. Mix to combine.
8) Pour half of the cream cheese mixture into the pumpkin mixture. Add evaporated milk to remaining cream cheese mixture.
9) Mix pumpkin mixture together and reserve ½ cup.
10) Pour pumpkin mixture into the crust. Completely covering the bottom.
11) Next, pour cream cheese mixture on top.
12) Spoon dollops of the ½ cup pumpkin mixture onto the top of the cheesecake. Use a butter knife to move it around the top creating swirls.
13) Bake for 1 hour. Turn oven off and let cool in oven for another hour. Once cooled, refrigerate for several hours or overnight.
14) Serve with fresh raspberries and enjoy!

Simple Mills products are non-GMO, naturally gluten free, grain free, soy free and corn free.

PUMPKIN CAKE POPS

Make any fall occasion pop with these fun-to-eat fall-themed cake pops! Made with *Simple Mills* pumpkin bread mix, they're the perfect portion size and look and taste delicious.

INGREDIENTS

1 package *Simple Mills* Pumpkin Bread Mix
1 cup *Simple Mills* Vanilla Frosting
1 cup white chocolate melting wafers
1 package treat sticks
Orange icing (optional)

Makes about 15 cake pops.

DIRECTIONS

1) Bake pumpkin bread according to package instructions for bread in a greased round cake pan.
2) Let cake cool completely and transfer to a medium bowl.
3) Have fun crumbling the cooled cake into pieces with your hands! Make sure there are no large lumps left.
4) Add the frosting into the mixed-up cake and using a spoon, mix together.
5) Roll the cake into balls (about 1 tablespoon per ball) and place on a baking sheet. Refrigerate for 2 hours or freeze for 1 hour.
6) Coat the cake pops: In a ball jar, melt the white chocolate according to package directions.
7) Flip an empty box you have laying around your house over so that the bottom is facing up and punch small wholes (the size of the treat sticks!) into it.
8) Remove 2-3 cake pops from the fridge at a time and begin coating.
9) Dip the treat stick into the white chocolate just so that the very tip is coated. Then push it halfway through the cake pop.
10) Dip cake pop into the ball jar so that the entire ball is covered. One dip that coats the entire ball is best for achieving an even looking coating.
11) Repeat with remaining cake pops and let them dry facing up in the box.
12) Once they have cooled completely (in about an hour) you can remove them from the box and lay them flat.
13) Coat the cake pops with a drizzle of orange icing, and enjoy!

PUMPKIN PIE SKILLET COBBLER

This gluten-free pumpkin pie cobbler is almost like an upside-down pumpkin pie with the crunch on top! The crumble on top gives it a nice nutty oat flavor of fall.

INGREDIENTS

For the cobbler:
3 eggs
1 can pumpkin puree
½ cup brown sugar
½ cup unsweetened almond milk
2 tsp. pumpkin pie spice
1 tsp. vanilla

For the topping:
½ cup walnuts, chopped
¼ cup gluten-free oats
5 tbsp. coconut oil
1 tsp. cinnamon
pinch of salt
sprinkle of nutmeg

DIRECTIONS

1) Preheat the oven to 375°F. Grease a skillet with coconut oil

2) In a medium bowl, whisk together sugar and eggs. Add pumpkin puree, almond milk, pumpkin pie spice and vanilla.

3) Once combined pour into prepared skillet.

4) In a small bowl, combine walnuts, oats, coconut oil, cinnamon, salt and nutmeg.

5) Top pumpkin mixture with walnut oat topping and bake for about 45 minutes.

Pumpkin Fact:

THE NAME PUMPKIN COMES FROM THE GREEK WORD 'PEPON,' MEANING 'LARGE MELON.'

PUMPKIN NUT BUTTER BLONDIES WITH A PUMPKIN GRANOLA CRUST

Nut butter, pumpkin and granola come together in the most delicious of ways for these pumpkin blondie bars that contain simple ingredients and are easy to make.

INGREDIENTS

1 cup almond flour
1/2 cup pumpkin puree
1 egg
1/2 almond butter
1/4 cup maple syrup or honey
2 tsp. pumpkin pie spice
1 tsp. baking soda
1/4 tsp. salt
2 tbsp. white chocolate chips
2 tbsp. coconut oil
2 cups your favorite pumpkin granola

Makes 12 bars

DIRECTIONS

1) Pre-heat the oven to 350°F. Line a square baking dish with parchment paper.

2) Place granola and coconut oil in a food processor and pulse until the granola resembles graham cracker crumbs.

3) Use your fingers to press granola into bottom of the pan and bake for 10 minutes.

4) Meanwhile, whisk almond flour, baking soda, pumpkin pie spice and salt in a medium bowl.

5) In a separate bowl, combine the wet ingredients. Then, add to the bowl of dry ingredients and mix together.

6) Remove granola from oven and pour mixture on top.

7) Melt white chocolate chips in the microwave or by double boiling and drop melted white chocolate on top of pumpkin batter.

8) Use a toothpick to make swirls in the batter.

9) Bake for 25 minutes until toothpick comes out clean.

PUMPKIN COOKIES

PUMPKIN PEANUT BUTTER CUPS

Stash these in your freezer and enjoy a sweet little pumpkin peanut butter treat all fall long! These pumpkin peanut butter cups satisfy that sweet tooth with minimal sugar, and added nutrition from the pumpkin.

INGREDIENTS

1 cup dark chocolate chips, dairy-free if preferred

1 cup creamy natural (unsweetened) peanut butter

½ cup pumpkin puree

1 tbsp pure maple syrup

1 tbsp coconut flour

Makes 18 mini cups

DIRECTIONS

1) Line a mini muffin pan with 9 mini liners or use a silicon pan without liners.

2) Melt the dark chocolate in a microwave safe bowl and microwave in 30 second increments until chocolate is melted.

3) Once chocolate is melted, add 1 teaspoon to the bottom of each cup (about 1 heaping teaspoon). Use the spoon to push/spread the chocolate all the way up sides of each liner, Place the pan in freezer for 5 minutes to harden the chocolate.

4) To make the pumpkin peanut butter mixture, add pumpkin puree, peanut butter, maple syrup and coconut flour to a medium bowl and mix until smooth, place ½ tablespoon of the mixture in each cup on top of the chocolate.

5) Place back in the freezer while you melt the remaining cup of chocolate in the microwave.

6) Spoon about 1 teaspoon on top of the pumpkin peanut butter mixture until covered.

7) Freeze for 10 minutes until chocolate is solid.

8) Store in the freezer in an airtight container and don't forget they are there!

ONCE UPON A PALEO PUMPKIN COOKIE

When you're craving all of that fall flavor, but none of the extra sugar found in fall treats, reach for these paleo pumpkin cookies---a cookie recipe that I make again and again and always enjoy as a better for you treat!

INGREDIENTS

1½ cup almond flour
¼ cup coconut flour
¼ cup pumpkin flour
¼ cup maple syrup
1 cup pumpkin puree
1 egg
1½ tsp. pumpkin pie spice
1 tbsp. coconut oil
2 tsp. vanilla extract
2 tsp. baking powder
½ tsp. baking soda
¼ tsp. salt

DIRECTIONS

1) Preheat the oven to 375°F.

2) In a medium bowl, whisk together almond, coconut and pumpkin flour. Add pumpkin pie spice, baking soda, baking powder, pumpkin pie spice, and salt.

3) In a small bowl, lightly whisk the egg and add pumpkin puree, maple syrup, melted coconut oil and vanilla extract.

4) Add the wet ingredients to the dry and mix until combined.

5) Using a cookie scoop or a tablespoon scoop the dough onto a cookie sheet. Bake cookies for 12 minutes until they appear a darker orange/ medium brown color.

6) Cool and enjoy!

Makes about 18 cookies.

THIN AND CRISPY PUMPKIN CHOCOLATE CHIP COOKIES

As thin and crispy as they get with a hint of fall—that's the way these cookies crumble! They're thin and crispy on the outside and soft and chewy in the inside thanks to the addition of creamy pumpkin puree.

INGREDIENTS

2¼ cup all-purpose flour
2½ stick unsalted butter, softened
1¼ cup sugar
½ cup brown sugar
¼ cup pumpkin puree
½ tsp. baking soda
1 tsp. salt
2 tsp. vanilla extract
2 tsp. pumpkin pie spice
2 eggs, room temp
1 cup chocolate chips

DIRECTIONS

1) Pre heat oven to 350°F.

2) In a medium bowl whisk together flour and baking soda.

3) In another bowl, beat butter with both sugars until fluffy. Beat in salt, vanilla and eggs until combined.

4) Mix in flour mixture until just combined. Fold in chocolate chips.

5) Using a cookie scoop drops scoops about 2 inches apart on a parchment lined baking sheet. They will spread!

6) Bake for 8-10 minutes until the cookies are golden around the edges but appear soft in the center.

7) Let cool completely on a wire rack and enjoy!

Makes about 3 dozen cookies.

I love stashing these in the freezer. They taste even better cold!

PILLOWY PUMPKIN CHOCOLATE CHIP COOKIES

Bask in the flavors of pumpkin, banana, and pumpkin pie spice with every bite of these gluten and dairy free pumpkin white chocolate chip cookies. Have one with your pumpkin coffee, or drizzled with pumpkin spice almond butter on top!

INGREDIENTS

2¼ cup gluten-free flour
1 tsp. salt
1 tsp. vanilla
1 tsp. baking soda
1 cup coconut oil, melted
¼ + 2 tbsp. brown sugar
1 medium very ripe banana, mashed
⅔ cup pumpkin puree
1 tbsp. ground flax seeds
3 tbsp. water
1 cup dairy free chocolate or white chocolate chips

DIRECTIONS

1) Preheat oven to 375°F.

2) In a large bowl, mix melted coconut oil and brown sugar until combined.

3) In a small bowl mash the banana until smooth. Add the flax seeds and water mixture.

4) Add the banana flax seed mixture to the larger bowl, along with the pumpkin and vanilla and mix together.

5) Sift flour, baking soda and salt, add to larger bowl and mix together until just combined.

6) Add white chocolate chips, and drop by the spoonful onto baking sheet.

7) Bake for 16 minutes, cool on wire rack, and enjoy!

Makes 18 cookies

Oats have a relatively unique nutrition profile compared to other whole grains.

PUMPKIN OAT BREAKFAST COOKIES

These savory pumpkin oat breakfast cookies are something you'll want to wake up to all fall long. The chewy, soft oats complement the taste of pumpkin and cranberry and finish with a pumpkin seed crunch. Your house will be filled with the aroma of autumn as they bake!

INGREDIENTS

1¼ cup Quaker Quick 1-Minute Gluten Free Oats
¼ hemp seeds
2 tbsp. dried cranberries
1 tbsp. chia seeds
2 tsp. baking powder
2 tsp. pumpkin pie spice
1 tsp. ginger
1 tsp. nutmeg
½ tsp. salt
¾ cup pumpkin puree
2 medium-sized eggs
½ cup unsweetened almond milk
3 tbsp. maple syrup
1 tbsp. almond butter
2 tsp. vanilla extract

DIRECTIONS

1) Pre-heat oven to 350°F.

2) Spray a rimmed baking sheet with cooking spray.

3) In a medium bowl, whisk together oat, hemp seeds, cranberries, chia seeds, baking powder, pumpkin pie spice, ginger, nutmeg and salt. Set aside.

4) In a separate medium-sized bowl, mix together pumpkin puree, eggs, almond milk, almond butter, maple syrup, and vanilla. Slowly stir into the dry ingredients.

5) Make sure everything is evenly incorporated, then add the pumpkin seeds.

6) Use a cookie scoop or a tablespoon to drop dough two inches apart on the baking sheet. Bake for 10 minutes then let cool completely on a cooling rack before serving.

Makes 15 cookies. Cookies can be stored in an airtight container in the fridge for about a week.

PUMPKIN SOUPS

"Pepita" means "little seeds of squash" in Spanish. They don't have a shell and are only found in select pumpkin varieties.

LEMONY PUMPKIN SOUP

This simple, yet satisfying savory pumpkin soup is easy to make and is sure to warm you up in chillier weather. The siggi's yogurt gives it its thick, creamy texture and is made with simple ingredients and not a lot of sugar.

INGREDIENTS

Soup

2½ cup low sodium vegetable broth
2 cups pumpkin puree
1 cup siggi's 4% whole-milk yogurt
¼ cup freshly squeezed lemon juice
1 tbsp. olive oil
2 cloves garlic, minced
1 shallot, diced
1½ tsp. freshly grated ginger
1 tsp. red pepper flakes
1 tsp. turmeric
Pinch of nutmeg
Salt & freshly ground pepper to taste

Pepita Parmesan Topping (optional)

¼ cup pepitas (green pumpkin seeds)
½ cup shredded parmesan cheese

Serves 4.

DIRECTIONS

1) In a soup pot over medium heat, add 1 tbsp olive oil, shallot and garlic. Cook for 2-3 minutes, or until translucent and fragrant.

2) Add the remaining ingredients, stir to combine, and bring to a light simmer for 10 minutes.

3) Transfer soup mixture to a blender or use an emulsion blender to puree the soup.

4) Pour soup back into pot and continue cooking for an additional 10 minutes.

5) For the pepita parmesan topping: pre-heat oven to 325°F. Place pepitas on one half of a baking sheet lined with parchment paper so none are on top of each other. Sprinkle a heaping tablespoon of parmesan cheese and pat down into circles on the other half of the pan. Repeat with remaining cheese. Bake for about 8-10 minutes until cheese is golden and crisp.

6) Pour soup into bowls and top with parmesan cheese crisps, pepitas and extra freshly ground black pepper if you desire!

Oats are a relatively powerful super grain and possess more possibilities than people think!

VEGGIE PUMPKIN OAT CHILI

This veggie pumpkin chili, made with Quaker oats, is the perfect thing is the perfect thing to warm you up on a chilly fall night—plus it's packed with veggies and the goodness of oats!

INGREDIENTS

2 tbsp extra virgin olive oil
2 cloves garlic, minced
1 shallot, diced
2¼ cup vegetable broth
1 15 oz. can pumpkin puree
1 can crushed, fire roasted tomatoes
1 can black beans
2 tbsp. chili powder
1 tbsp. red pepper flakes
1 tbsp. dried oregano
2 tbsp. corn starch
1 cup Quaker Steel Cut Oats
salt and pepper to taste

DIRECTIONS

1) Heat the olive oil in a large soup pot over medium-high heat. Add the shallot, garlic, and mushrooms, and cook until just tender and fragrant, about 4 minutes.

2) Add the vegetable broth, pumpkin puree, tomatoes, black beans, chili powder, ginger, crushed red pepper, and oregano.

3) Stir and bring to a boil. Then reduce heat, add cornstarch, and let simmer for 25 minutes.

4) When you've got 4-5 minutes left, stir in oats.

5) Season to taste with salt and pepper and top with fresh cilantro, or sage, sliced avocado or jalapeño for a spicy kick.

Serves 4

PUMPKIN MAIN DISHES

Gilbert's Craft Sausages are all natural with no artificial nitrites, or nitrates, and made with antibiotic-free chicken. They come individually wrapped for extra convienence!

PUMPKIN SAUSAGE FRITATTA

Pumpkin in a frittata? Yes I did! Pumpkin adds a hint of orange and a smooth texture to this frittata made with Gilbert's Craft Sausages.

INGREDIENTS

8 large eggs
1 package Gilbert's Craft Sausages Bourbon Apple Chicken Sausage
½ cup shredded cheddar cheese
½ cup red and orange peppers, thinly sliced
½ cup cooked potatoes, cubed
¼ cup pumpkin puree
½ tsp. crushed red pepper flakes
salt and pepper to taste
avocado slices for topping

DIRECTIONS

1) Pre-heat oven to 375°F.

2) In a medium bowl, whisk eggs, pumpkin puree, red pepper, and salt and pepper.

3) Unwrap 3 sausage links and cut into thin slices.

4) Add veggies, and sausage slices to egg mixture.

5) Pour egg mixture into a lightly greased skillet.

6) Bake for 20 minutes, or until the edges appear golden brown and the eggs in the center are set.

7) Let cool, and cut into slices. Top with sliced avocado and enjoy!

Makes about 8 pieces

Beta-carotene, which gives pumpkins their orange color, is a free-radical fighting antioxidant. Our bodies convert beta-carotene into vitamin A, which is essential for skin, eye and immune health.

PUMPKIN RAVIOLI IN A BURNT BROWN BUTTER SAUCE WITH CRISPY SAGE AND TOASTED PINE NUTS

This recipe is like fall in a bowl! Not only does it look like an autumn landscape when plated, but each bite of pumpkin, toasted pine nuts, pumpkin seeds and crispy sage will remind you of your favorite things about the season!

INGREDIENTS

3 eggs
1 cup all-purpose flour
pinch of salt & pepper
1 cup LIBBY'S® 100% Pure Pumpkin
½ cup part-skim ricotta cheese
½ tsp. cayenne pepper
½ tsp. salt
1 tsp. red pepper flakes
1 tbsp. butter, metled
pinch of nutmeg
1 cup cooked butternut squash, cubed
8 sage leaves
¼ cup pine nuts
¼ cup pepitas
¼ cup shredded parmesan cheese

DIRECTIONS

For the ravioli:

1) In a food processor, add eggs, salt and pepper and pulse.

2) Add half of flour, pulse and add the rest. Continue to pulse until dough comes together (about 1 minute). If dough is overly sticky, continue to add more flour, 1 tablespoon at a time until texture softens.

3) Remove dough and roll into two equal balls. Cover and refrigerate dough for 30 minutes.

4) Remove dough from fridge. Using a pasta roller, feed dough through roller until paper thin consistency. Note, depending on pasta roller this will take multiple rolls through settings of the tool.

5) Lay sheet of thin dough flat on a flat surface. Place 1/2 tbsp. of filling onto dough. Repeat until you have a row of filling on the dough about 3 inches apart from each other.

(Continued...)

7) Using a ravioli stamper, stamp around each pocket of filling. Repeat with remaining dough.

8) Bring a pot of lightly salted water to a vigorous boil. Slowly add the ravioli and let cook for about 4 minutes.

9) Using a slotted spoon, remove the ravioli and place on a plate not on top of each other.

For the filling:

1) Combine pumpkin, ricotta, cayenne pepper, melted butter, salt and nutmeg in a small bowl.

To assemble:

1) In a medium skillet over medium-low heat, melt the butter and add the pine nuts and pumpkin seeds. Add butternut squash and sage. Stir together gently.

2) Add 3-4 ravioli at a time. Mix them around the pan so that they are gently coated in the different flavors.

3) Plate and top with Parmesan cheese.

Makes 2 dozen ravioli.

PUMPKIN MEATBALLS IN A PUMPKIN SPICED TOMATO SAUCE

Pumpkin puree puts a seasonal twist on these turkey meatballs, and adds nutrition and flavor to every bite! These meatballs are great to pair with spaghetti squash for a dinner bursting with vitamin A!

INGREDIENTS

For the meatballs:
1¼ lbs ground turkey
½ cup pumpkin puree
¼ cup almond flour
¾ tsp salt
1 tsp black pepper
½ tsp. crushed red pepper
1 large egg
1 tsp fresh or dried thyme
1 tbsp fresh sage

For the Pumpkin-Spiced Tomato Sauce:
2 tbsp olive oil
1 cup pumpkin puree
1 cup your favorite tomato sauce
¼ cup coconut mik
½ cup chicken broth
1 clove garlic minced
2 tsp Italian seasoning
2 tsp pumpkin pie spice
1 tsp sage
Salt and pepper to taste

DIRECTIONS

1) Preheat oven to 425 degrees F and line a baking sheet with parchment paper.

2) Mix all meatball ingredients in a large bowl with your hands until well combined.

3) Use your hands to roll meat into balls and add to baking sheet.

4) Bake meatballs for 17 minutes.

5) In the meantime, prepare sauce by adding the olive oil to a large saucepan or stock pot over medium heat.

6) Add the garlic and cook until fragrant.

7) Lower the heat, then add the tomato sauce, pumpkin, broth, coconut milk, Italian

(continued)

seasoning, pumpkin pie spice, sage, dried rosemary and stir to combine well.
Add the salt and pepper.

8) Cover and allow to simmer for 5 minutes before adding the meatballs. Adding the meatballs and simmer for 5 more minutes.

9) Garnish with additional sage and Parmesan cheese. Serve and enjoy!

Prep Time: 15 minutes
Cook Time: 25 minutes
Total Time: 40 minutes

Makes 18 meatballs

Top spaghetti squash with pumpkin meatballs for a delicious dinner that is high in vitamin A and bursting will fall flavor.

Net Wt 9.8oz (277g)

HARVEST SALAD PIZZA

Take a bite out of fall with this autumn inspired pizza made on *Simple Mills* pizza dough.

INGREDIENTS

1 package *Simple Mills* gluten-free pizza dough
2 tbsp. pumpkin seed pesto (see page 109 for recipe)
1 tbsp. olive oil
1 cup cubed pumpkin or butternut squash
1 bunch lacinato kale, washed and destemmed
1 tsp. red pepper flakes
½ cup shredded parmesan cheese
¼ cup dried cranberries
¼ cup pepitas
salt and pepper to taste

DIRECTIONS

1) Prepare pizza dough according to package instructions.

2) Place kale in a small bowl, drizzle olive oil on top, add red pepper flakes and massage until the kale feels soft.

3) Spread pumpkin seed pesto onto the pizza crust and top with kale, cubed pumpkin, cranberries, pepitas, parmesan cheese and salt and pepper.

4) Finish baking according to package instructions, cut into slices and enjoy!

Makes 2 individual pizzas.

Simple Mills believes in clean, nutritious food for a better life—it's that simple.

Simple Mills are available on Amazon and in Jewel Osco and Target.

PUMPKIN SEED CRUSTED SALMON

Get an extra dose of healthy omega-3 fatty acids with this salmon and pumpkin seed combination! The seeds give the salmon a nutritious and crunchy coating, and together it's great ontop of salads or with seasonal veggies!

INGREDIENTS

2 wild caught salmon filets
½ cup pumpkin seeds, finely chopped
1 egg
1 tbsp. honey
2 tsp. red pepper flakes
salt and pepper to taste

DIRECTIONS

1) Pre-heat oven to 375°F and line a shallow baking dish with parchment paper.

2) In a shallow bowl, whisk the egg, add the honey, red pepper flakes and salt and pepper.

3) Drudge the salmon (skin side up) through the egg mixture than press down into the pumpkin seeds, evenly coating the top.

4) Bake for 15-17 minutes.

Makes 2 servings

Pumpkin Fact:

PUMPKINS ARE 90% WATER. ONE CUP OF CANNED PUMPKIN ONLY HAS 83 CALORIES AND ONLY HALF A GRAM OF FAT.THEY ALSO HAVE MORE FIBER THAN KALE, MORE POTASSIUM THAN BANANAS AND ARE FULL OF HEART-HEALTHY MAGNESIUM AND IRON.

DAIRY-FREE PUMPKIN MAC & CHEESE

Warm up on a chilly fall night with this oh so creamy, dairy-free pumpkin mac and cheese! Made with LIBBY'S® 100% Pure Pumpkin and CARNATION® Almond Cooking Milk, the sauce is full of flavor and adds extra nutrition to this pasta dish you'll have on repeat all throughout the fall months.

INGREDIENTS

1½ cup LIBBY'S® 100% Pure Pumpkin
½ cup CARNATION® Almond Cooking Milk
1 tbsp. vegetable broth
2 tbsp. nutritional yeast
1 tbsp. maple syrup
2 tsp. olive oil
1 clove garlic
1 tsp. red pepper flakes (extra if you want a spicier sauce!)
pinch of salt and pepper

DIRECTIONS

1) In a blender, combine pumpkin and the rest of the ingredients until a smooth texture appears.

2) Transfer sauce to a small saucepan and heat over medium low.

3) Combine with cooked pasta of your choice. Add spinach or other vegetables. Top with fresh sage and enjoy!

Serves 2

Replace 1 egg with 1/4 cup pumpkin puree in recipes to make them dairy free and extra moist. Whether you have dairy restrictions or simply prefer non-dairy milk, you can make your recipes richer and creamier by adding new CARNATION® dairy-free Almond Cooking Milk.

PUMPKIN SHASHUKA

Shakshuka is a traditional Middle Eastern breakfast dish that gets a pumpkin spin in this recipe perfect for fall brunches!

INGREDIENTS

1 cup pumpkin puree
1 can fire roasted tomatoes
2 tbsp. olive oil
4 eggs
2 cloves garlic, minced
1 tsp. ground cumin
1 tsp. paprika
⅛ tsp. cayenne
½ tsp. ground ginger
1 tsp. salt
¾ cup feta cheese, crumbled
chopped cilantro and lightly toasted pine nuts for topping

DIRECTIONS

1) Preheat oven to 375°F.

2) In a medium skillet, heat olive oil over medium-low heat, add minced garlic and sauté until fragrant.

3) Stir in cumin, paprika, cayenne and ginger and then add tomatoes and pumpkin puree.

4) Simmer until mixture begins to thicken and season with salt and pepper.

5) Remove from heat and sprinkle crumbled feta on top of mixture.

6) Gently crack the eggs into the tomato pumpkin mixture, leaving a little space between each one.

7) Transfer skillet to the oven and bake until the eggs are just set, about 10 minutes.

8) Top with toasted pine nuts, cilantro and hot sauce for a spicy kick!

PUMPKIN PIES

PUMPKIN SPICE LATTE PIE

This pie is the perfect homemade dessert to bring to Friendsgiving! Gluten-free, and extra crunchy from the granola crust, it's sure to be a crowd pleaser!

INGREDIENTS

For the crust:

1 package pumpkin granola (one of my favorites is Purely Elizabeth's pumpkin cinnamon flavor!)
2 tbsp. butter or coconut oil

For the filling:

1 can pumpkin puree
¼ cup maple syrup
¼ cup brewed coffee
¼ cup unsweetened almond milk
1 tbsp. coconut oil
2½ tsp. cornstarch
2 tsp. pumpkin pie spice
½ tsp. espresso powder
¼ tsp. salt

DIRECTIONS

1) To make the crust, pre-heat the oven to 325°F, and place entire package granola in a food processor. Pulse until granola resembles graham cracker crumbs.

2) Pour into a small bowl and add butter or coconut oil. Mix until incorporated.

3) Pour granola mixture into a pie pan and use your fingers to pack it into the bottom and up the sides.

4) Bake for 10 minutes.

5) Meanwhile, make the filling by mixing together all of the remaining ingredients. It should appear a burnt orange color.

6) Turn up your oven to 350°F. Pour filling into granola pie crust and bake for 50 minutes.

7) Slice and serve with whipped cream, and or a sprinkle of pumpkin pie spice!

Makes 1 pie

BARB'S PUMPKIN SPICE JELLO PIE

Ever since I can remember my mom has been making this pie with strawberry jello that we like to call "pink cake". I put a pumpkin spin on it by using pumpkin spice gelatin and that paired with the graham cracker crust makes it not only perfect and delicious for any fall occasion, but ever so simple to make!

INGREDIENTS

1 package pumpkin spice gelatin
1 container whipped topping
⅔ cup hot water
1 cup ice cubes
1 pre-made graham cracker pie crust

DIRECTIONS

1) In a small bowl dissolve one package of pumpkin spice gelatin in ⅔ cup hot water. Mix for exactly 2 minutes until all the gelatin is dissolved.

2) Add 1 cup ice cubes and mix for exactly 2 minutes more.

3) After 2 minutes takes the ice cubes out even if they are not fully dissolved.

4) Add in whole container of whipped topping. Mix for 1-2 minutes until completely incorporated in gelatin mixture.

5) Place in the fridge to thicken for 10 -15 minutes.

6) Remove from fridge and pour into graham cracker pie crust.

7) Let set in fridge overnight, cut into pieces and topped with additional whipped cream and pumpkin pie spice is desired!

Makes one 8-piece pie

PUMPKIN SIDES

Freeze pesto in an ice cube tray to use all throughout the season

PUMPKIN SEED PESTO

Pumpkin seeds, AKA pepitas, are full of flavor, not to mention rich in antioxidants and the minerals iron, zinc and magnesium! Their buttery texture contributes to the rich taste of this pesto, which is great to use on pastas, vegetables or simply on savory toast this fall.

INGREDIENTS

2 cups arugula
1 cup basil
⅔ cup pepitas
½ cup parmesan cheese
2 tbsp. pine nuts
¼ cup extra virgin olive oil
3 cloves garlic
2 tbsp. water
1 tsp. red pepper flakes
½ tsp. salt
½ tsp. freshly ground black pepper

DIRECTIONS

1) Heat a skillet to medium-low and toast pumpkin seeds and pine nuts until fragrant and golden brown (stir frequently or constantly).

2) In a food processor add garlic and pulse until garlic is minced.

3) Add the toasted pumpkin seeds and pine nuts, arugula, parmesan, red pepper flakes and salt and pepper.

4) With the processor on, stream in the olive oil and water. Add more olive if you'd like a thinner pesto. Use within a week, or freeze pesto in an ice cube tray to use all throughout the season.

Pumpkin Fact:

PEPITAS ARE PUMPKIN SEEDS THAT GROW SHELL-FREE IN CERTAIN TYPES OF PUMPKINS.

PUMPKIN & TURMERIC HUMMUS

This pumpkin hummus embodies autumn with a bright pumpkin-y flavor! Pair it with crackers, carrots, cucumbers and enjoy it's lemon tartness and mild touch of heat.

INGREDIENTS

1 13 oz can chickpeas, drained and rinsed with shells removed
¼ cup extra-virgin olive oil
⅔ cup pumpkin puree
2 cloves garlic
2 tbsp. tahini
the juice of a small lemon, squeezed
½ tsp. turmeric
1 tsp. crushed red pepper
½ tsp. salt
½ tsp. pepper
optional garnish: olive oil, toasted pine nuts, pumpkin seeds, cilantro, & sage

DIRECTIONS

1) Peel the garlic cloves and place in a food processor to mince.

2) Add the deshelled chickpeas, pumpkin, tahini, lemon juice, turmeric, red pepper flakes, salt and pepper and pulse until combined.

3) Pour in the olive oil and continue pulsing until silky smooth.

4) Place in a small bowl and top with a drizzle of olive oil, toasted pine nuts and pumpkin seeds and sage or cilantro if you wish.

Makes 1½ cups hummus

Removing the shells of the garbanzo beans is the key to smooth, creamy hummus!

When you see a can of Libby's® 100% Pure Pumpkin, you're practically looking at a pumpkin fresh from the patch. Libby's pumpkins go from farm to can in just a few hours so that fresh-from-the-farm flavor shines through in everything you put it in!

SWEET & SPICED PUMPKIN HUMMUS

Dip apple slices or crackers into this sweet pumpkin hummus and prepare to taste the quintessential flavors of fall! With hints of maple syrup, cinnamon, vanilla and almond, it's the perfect dip to bring to any fall get together.

INGREDIENTS

1 13 oz can chickpeas, drained and rinsed with shells removed
1 cup LIBBY'S® 100% Pure Pumpkin
2 tsp. vanilla extract
2 tbsp. almond butter
3 tbsp. maple syrup
1 tbsp. olive oil
2 tsp. pumpkin pie spice
1 tsp. cinnamon
pinch of nutmeg
pinch of salt
1 tbsp. honey and pumpkin seeds for drizzle on top

Yields 1½ cups hummus

DIRECTIONS

1. Combine de-shelled chickpeas, pumpkin, almond butter, maple syrup, and olive oil in a food processor until a smooth and creamy texture begins to appear.

2. Add the pumpkin pie spice, nutmeg, salt, and add vanilla extract 1 tsp. at a time and continue pulsing.

3. Once hummus appears extra thick and smooth, transfer to bowl and garnish with a drizzle of honey, and pumpkin seeds.

SPICY PUMPKIN FONDUE

Get your friends together and dip into the flavors of the season with this cheesy pumpkin fondue!

INGREDIENTS

¾ cup grated Gruyere
1 cup half & half
½ cup pumpkin puree
2 tsp. freshly ground black pepper
sprinkle of nutmeg
pinch of salt

DIRECTIONS

1) In a small saucepan over low heat, add a quarter of the half & half and all of the cheese.

2) Stir and slowly add the rest of the half & half in and the pumpkin.

3) Continue stirring and season with black pepper, nutmeg and salt.

4) Turn off the heat, and let mixture thicken for a few more minutes.

5) Use as a dipping sauce for raw veggies, crackers and more.

Makes 1 cup

Bake this fondue in a pumpkin for an extra special Halloween party appetizer.

once
Upon
a
PUMPKIN

PUMPKIN SEEDS 5 WAYS

PUMPKIN SEEDS 5 WAYS

General directions to start with for seeds:

1) Preheat oven to 350°F. Line a baking sheet with parchment paper.

2) Separate the seeds from the pulp of your pumpkin. Dry them off with a paper town if especially moist. Combine 1 cup pumpkin seeds with 2 tbsp. coconut oil, coat with one of the seasonings below, roast for 20 minutes and enjoy!

PUMPKIN PIE SPICE + COLLAGEN PUMPKIN SEEDS SEASONING

Combine one scoop of collagen peptides and 1 tsp. pumpkin pie spice to pumpkin seeds, mix together and roast.

VANILLA + CINNAMON SEASONING

Combine 2 tsp. vanilla extract and 2 tsp. cinnamon, add to pumpkin seeds, mix together and roast.

MATCHA COCONUT SEASONING

Combine 1 tbsp. matcha and 1 tbsp. unsweetened coconut flakes, add to pumpkin seeds, mix together and roast.

TURMERIC + BLACK PEPPER SEASONING

Combine one scoop of collagen peptides and 1 tsp. pumpkin pie spice to pumpkin seeds, mix together and roast.

BBQ SEASONING

Combine 2 tbsp. brown sugar, 1 tbsp. sea salt, 2 tsp. freshly ground black pepper, 2 tsp. paprika, 2 tsp. garlic powder, 2 tsp. onion powder, 1 tsp. ginger, 1/2 tsp. cayenne powder, add to pumpkin seeds, mix together and roast.

Pumpkin Pie Spice & Collagen Pumpkin Seeds

Turmeric and black pepper have key active ingredients that contribute to each other's anti-inflammatory, antioxidant and disease-fighting qualities. Be sure to combine both to reap the nutritional benefits!

On average, pumpkins have about 500 seeds.

The Irish brought the tradition of carving pumpkins into Jack O'Lantern to America. But, the original Jack O'Lantern was not a pumpkin because they didn't exist in Ireland. Ancient Celtic cultures in Ireland carved turnips, potatoes, and beets.

Matcha promotes an alert calmness and pumpkin seeds are a good source of protein, so grab these as an afternoon snack when you need to power through the rest of the day!

PUMPKIN DRINKS

ONCE UPON A DRUNKEN PUMPKIN

Spice up your night with this boozy pumpkin cocktail. The flavors of pumpkin pie spice and nutmeg pair with rum

INGREDIENTS

2 ounces Captain Morgan Jack-O'Blast Rum (can sub any other rum you have on hand)
¼-inch piece ginger, peeled
1 tbsp. pumpkin butter
1 tbsp. lime juice
½ tsp. pumpkin pie spice
couple ice cubes
nutmeg to garnish

DIRECTIONS

1) In a cocktail shaker muddle ginger, and add rum, pumpkin butter, orange juice, lime juice, pumpkin pie spice and ice.

2) Shake and strain into a glass.

3) Garnish with and apple slice and enjoy!

PUMPKIN BANANA SMOOTHIE

On days when the seasons are just changing from summer to fall ever so subtly enjoy the best of both worlds with this pumpkin spice smoothie! It's all the fall flavor you could want in a refreshing smoothie you'll want to make again and again!

INGREDIENTS

1 cup unsweetened almond milk, oat, or cashew milk
1 medium banana
¼ cup pumpkin puree
1 tbsp. hemp seeds
1 tsp. freshly grated ginger
2 tsp. flax seeds
2 tsp. pumpkin pie spice
½ cup ice

DIRECTIONS

1) Combine all of the ingredients in a blender until blended smooth.

Pumpkin Fact:

PUMPKIN PUREE OUT OF THE CAN WILL LAST FOR 1 WEEK IN THE FRIDGE AND UP TO 3 MONTHS IN THE FREEZER

PUMPKIN GREEN SMOOTHIE

Pumpkin puree can thicken your smoothies and an extra nutrition without you even knowing it's there! This green smoothie is refreshing with a creamy texture and bursting with vitamin C from the pumpkin, spinach and lemon!

INGREDIENTS

1 cup unsweetened almond milk
2 handfuls of spinach
¼ cup pumpkin puree
the juice from 1/2 of a lemon
1 tbsp. hemp seeds
2 tsp. freshly grated ginger
½ cup ice

DIRECTIONS

1) In a blender, combine all of the ingredients and mix until smooth.

Pumpkin Fact:

95% OF THE PUMPKINS GROWN IN THE UNITED STATES ARE GROWN IN ILLINOIS.

PUMPKIN DOG TREATS

PUMPKIN PEANUT BUTTER DOG TREATS

Did you know pumpkin is is also good for your pooch? Yes, that's right! Pumpkin can help relieve tummy troubles for your dog and they love the taste too! Your four-legged friend is sure to love this delicious treats--my dog Pumpkin sure does!

INGREDIENTS

½ cup pumpkin puree
¼ cup pumpkin flour (can sub coconut flour)
1 tbsp. coconut oil
1 egg
½ of a banana, mashed
1 tbsp. peanut butter
1 tsp. cinnamon
pinch of nutmeg

DIRECTIONS

1) Preheat oven to 325°F.

2) In a bowl combine, pumpkin, pumpkin flour, coconut oil, egg, banana, peanut butter, cinnamon and nutmeg.

3) Use a small pumpkin shaped cookie cutter to cut pumpkin shapes out of dough or use dog bone shaped baking pan.

4) Bake for 30 minutes and let cool completely. Store in an airtight container in the fridge.

This past spring we welcomed Pumpkin the Cavalier King Charles Spaniel into our lives! He is truly as sweet as pumpkin pie and true to his name, enjoyed these treats very much!

Made in the USA
Middletown, DE
05 November 2018